CCSS Genre Tall Tale

Essential Question
What kinds of stories do we tell?
Why do we tell them?

An Extraordinary Girl

BY ALI MACKISACK
ILLUSTRATED BY SARA BENECINO

CHAPTER 1

An Amazing Baby

Two hundred years ago, an astonishing baby was born. Ma and Pa Whirlwind already had nine boys, so they were surprised to find themselves blessed with a baby girl.

"She's amazing!" her happy parents cried. "We'll call her Sally Ann."

But the nine brothers were not so thrilled about having a baby girl in their family. They had all been hoping for another brother. Then they would have had even numbers for their team-wrestling, mountain-racing, waterfall-diving, and tree-climbing contests.

They were even less excited when Sally Ann opened her mouth and cried for the first time. That baby girl hollered so loudly that the thunder clapped in surprise. The noise knocked the head feathers off all the eagles in the entire state.

The brothers picked themselves up off the ground. The force of their baby sister's first holler had knocked them over in a pile.

"I wouldn't call her Sally Ann," the youngest brother muttered. "Thunder Ann is more like it."

And so that hollering infant became known as Sally Ann Thunder Ann Whirlwind.

It soon became clear that hollering was not Sally Ann Thunder Ann's only extraordinary talent.

When she was just two months old, she learned to walk. By that evening, she could run.

The next day, the brothers were having a mountain race. Sally Ann shot past them as they huffed and puffed up the slope. When she got to the top, she danced a jig. Sally Ann passed them again on the way back down, carrying a mountain goat in one hand and a jackrabbit in the other. She had decided she wanted them as pets.

When she was four months old, Sally Ann learned to swim. In a waterfall-diving competition with her brothers, Sally Ann dived over every waterfall and then swam back up them again. On the way, she caught enough perch to feed the family for a whole week.

When she was six months old, Sally Ann could scoot up and down the tallest trees before her brothers had even reached the lowest branches. Sometimes she would carry her daddy's 20-pound ax in one hand and cut the tree into kindling on the way down.

And by the time she was one year old, Sally Ann could out-wrestle every one of her brothers and every bear cub that wasn't afraid to wrestle her, too.

On her first birthday, Sally Ann's brothers finally admitted that she was indeed amazing, just as her parents had said on the day she was born.

"That's right," said Sally Ann as she blew out her birthday candle just by fluttering her eyelashes. "My name is Sally Ann Thunder Ann Whirlwind! I can out-holler, out-run, out-swim, out-climb, and out-wrestle any boy or girl in Kentucky. Just watch me!"

And that was no exaggeration! By the time she was ten years old, she had out-done and out-shone just about everyone in the state in virtually every test of strength there ever was.

So Sally Ann Thunder Ann Whirlwind decided the time had come to set off into the wilderness to see what she could see.

Sally Ann liked being on her own. She went where she wanted and did whatever took her fancy.

But Sally Ann did not enjoy the cold winters. Eventually, she took to doing what nature suggested. She slept the winters away curled up in a cozy den with the biggest, hairiest bear she could find.

One spring, though, she was so comfortable that she did not wake up before the bear did. When that bear woke up and found a human girl curled up beside him, oh, how he roared!

Sally Ann did not take too kindly to being awakened in such a rough and sudden way. She came out of her sleep as grumpy as a hive of bees poked with a stick and pounded by a storm.

She stared at the big bear for about five seconds, and then she commenced roaring right back at him. That bear's roar was loud enough to cause an avalanche half a mountainside away, but it had nothing on Sally Ann's. Her roar sent the falling stars shooting back up into the sky and the rivers running back to where they came from. Her roar was so loud it scared the bearskin clean off the bear's back.

"Excellent!" said Sally Ann. She picked up the bearskin and wrapped it around her shoulders. That bearskin kept her warm for many a frozen winter.

CHAPTER 2

Sally Ann Meets Davy Crockett

Sometimes Sally Ann felt an itsy bit lonely wandering through the woods all on her own, but she never had much time for the folk she met on her wandering way. She figured most of them weren't half as interesting or smart as the critters she knew in the woods.

Then one day while she was wandering along happy as you please, collecting rattlesnakes for hair ribbons, she came across an unusual sight. There, stuck in the crook of an oak tree, were a man's buckskin pants with a pair of buckskin moccasins underneath them. "Could it be some kind of newfangled bear trap?" Sally Ann wondered. "It isn't much like the old-fashioned ones."

She snapped a branch off an old hickory tree as easily as snapping a toothpick and gave the pants a good poke. Suddenly the pants came to life. They twisted and thrashed like a sackful of snakes, and the moccasins kicked like the back legs of a mule that's poked its head into a skunk hole.

Boy, did those pants let out a yell! They yelled so loud that the panthers in those parts turned from black to white and back again. Sally Ann was so impressed that she gave the pants another poke just to hear them holler one more time.

Then she walked around to the other side of the oak tree. A man's head was sticking out the other side of the crook. It looked as if the man had somehow gotten stuck there and had just about turned himself inside out and upside down and through his own middle trying to get free.

"Hmmm," mused Sally Ann, chewing thoughtfully on a piece of poison ivy. "Seems to me, stranger, you're snagged in there snugger than a snapping turtle's snout. You're more stuck than a skeeter in molasses. You're going to need my help, I reckon."

The man in the tree did not like the way this girl was making fun of him. He tried to look at her, but his head was facing the ground, and when he rolled his eyes up toward her, he just found himself staring at the inside of his own head.

"I surely do need some help, sweetie," said the man. "So why don't you run along and fetch your pa and tell him to bring his big ol' ax. Make it lickety-split, now, and I'll give you a pretty little ribbon for your hair."

Well, Sally Ann gave a snort of laughter.

"I don't need a ribbon, and I don't need some dang-fool old woodcutter calling me sweetie either," she said. "I'll help you just to stop your hollering. But then you better run out of my sight lickety-split!"

She pulled the crook open just enough so the man could raise his head—but he was still stuck tight.

Well, the man stuck in that there tree was none other than the heroic frontiersman Davy Crockett himself. The moment he had his first glimpse of Sally Ann Thunder Ann Whirlwind, he wanted her for his wife. And with every move she made to free him, he fell deeper in love.

Sally Ann was still riled. "Pretty ribbon indeed," she mumbled, unhooking the rattlesnakes from her braids and tying them into a rope. "I'd rather wear my old hornet's-nest hat!"

She threw her rattlesnake rope over one of the branches that still pinned Davy's head in the tree.

"Fetch my pa, you say?" she muttered. "I can swallow a thunderbolt and spit out the pieces. I can wring enough water out of a cactus to make a river a hundred miles long. I reckon I can do this without my pa."

She pulled down on the rattlesnake rope. "Make it lickety-split, my foot," she grumbled. "Why, I can run so fast I meet myself coming back." And then Davy was free.

The blood rushed from Davy Crockett's head as he stood upright at last and looked at his rescuer.

"I never met a gal like you before," he said. "I reckon we should get married."

Sally Ann opened her mouth to tell this fresh fellow exactly what she thought of his crazy-fool idea. But then Davy flashed his famous lightning grin at her, and for the first time in her life, she went weak at the knees.

"Oh—all right," she said, "but never call me sweetie, sweetie." She sauntered off to fetch her favorite hat, an eagle's nest with a wolf's tail for a feather, to wear at their wedding. She looked right pretty as she posed for their wedding photograph, too!

CHAPTER 3

Sally Ann Meets Mike Fink

Well, Sally Ann Thunder Ann Whirlwind Crockett and Davy Crockett were mighty happy together, and Sally Ann continued to impress her husband with her extraordinary ways. He was really proud of her, and he liked to boast about her to everyone he met.

Most people loved to hear of Davy and Sally Ann's entertaining exploits, but there was one man who didn't believe that anything Davy said was true. That man was Mike Fink.

Mike Fink was the king of the boatmen on the Mississippi River, and he was a bully. He boasted that he could out-run, out-jump, and out-fight any man on both sides of the river. He didn't like the sound of this Sally Ann Thunder Ann Whirlwind Crockett, so he decided to frighten her back into the hills she had come from.

The next time Mike Fink came across Davy Crockett telling tales of his wife's amazing adventures and courageous deeds, he laid down a wager. He bet Davy Crockett that he could scare Sally Ann so badly that her teeth would come loose and her toenails would fall out. If he lost the bet, he promised to catch Sally Ann a dozen wildcats.

Davy Crockett knew that trying to scare Sally Ann was like trying to open a barn door by throwing feathers at it. With a smile, he agreed to the wager. Then he went home right away to build a pen for the wildcats.

Now, Mike Fink was not only a boatman, he was also a champion alligator wrestler. So one day after he had killed a gigantic bull alligator, he took that alligator's skin and stitched himself inside it. Then he went and hid himself behind a log down where Sally Ann took a walk each night looking for porcupine quills for her hairbrush.

When Sally Ann came near, Mike leaped out at her and roared. He roared so loudly that he nearly scared himself out of that alligator suit, but Sally Ann barely paused. She shot that critter a look so cold it would have turned the smoke from a prairie fire to ice. Then she just carried on hunting for quills.

Mike Fink was none too happy about this. Leaping up to make the alligator walk on its hind legs, he began roaring louder than ever. He advanced on Sally Ann with his claws outstretched.

This time, Sally Ann shot him a look so sharp it punched holes in the sky for the stars. Then she turned her back on him. She took out a toothpick she had made from a tree branch and started cleaning her teeth and humming a little song.

Mike Fink couldn't believe it. With his loudest roar yet, he leaped toward Sally Ann as if he were about to take a huge bite out of her.

Well, if Sally Ann Thunder Ann Whirlwind Crockett hated anything more than being called sweetie, it was having a bite taken out of her by an alligator. She swiped at the head of the loathsome creature with her toothpick.

That toothpick cut the head clean off Mike Fink's alligator suit, taking most of the hair on Mike Fink's head with it, and flung it across the state. When she saw that it was Mike Fink inside that alligator suit, Sally Ann's anger rolled in like a Mississippi flood.

She flung down her toothpick, lifted Mike Fink out of the suit, and held him by the ears. She began to twirl him around and around her head, and as she twirled him, every one of his toenails flew off.

When he was dizzier than a flock of turkeys in a twister, Sally Ann let him go. He flew though the air and landed five miles upriver with every tooth loose.

Davy Crockett found Mike Fink in a terrible way the next morning. Mike told Davy he had been swallowed whole by a giant alligator and had fought himself free using only a toothpick.

But Davy Crockett knew better. The next day, there were a dozen snarling, spitting wildcats in Sally Ann's pet pen. It didn't take her long to sort those little kitties out.

And so the Crocketts lived happily for years, raising wild children and gentle wildcats. Then Davy had to go to Congress, leaving Sally Ann to deal with a gang of bull alligators ... but that's another story, and a tale so tall you probably wouldn't believe it anyway.

Respond to Reading

Summarize

Use the most important details from the story to summarize *An Extraordinary Girl*. Your graphic organizer may help you.

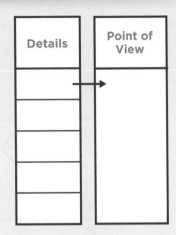

Details	Point of View

Text Evidence

1. How do you know that *An Extraordinary Girl* is a tall tale? Give details about the characters and events. **GENRE**

2. How does the narrator regard Sally Ann Thunder Ann Whirlwind? Give several examples of descriptions that show this. **POINT OF VIEW**

3. What does the word *newfangled* mean on page 7? Use context clues and an antonym from the paragraph to help you. **SYNONYMS AND ANTONYMS**

4. Write about the narrator's view of Mike Fink. **WRITE ABOUT READING**

Compare Texts

Read a legend about a very determined frog.

How Coqui Got Her Song

Everything on the island of Puerto Rico looked beautiful, but Paz the parrot, head of the forest, was worried. It was quiet—too quiet.

All the birds were dozing instead of shrieking in the treetops as they used to. Lizard was basking on a warm rock instead of pattering through the undergrowth. Snake hung limply from a branch, and Toad sunned himself on the riverbank. There was no slithering or hopping or plopping. Even the tiny, silent tree frog, Coqui (*ko-KEE*), lazed and lolled the peaceful days away.

Paz wanted their island to bustle with sound and movement, but she saw that the creatures were getting lazier by the day. "I must think of something to get them moving again," she thought.

The next morning, Paz screeched out the call for a forest meeting. The creatures straggled in. Snake slithered sleepily, and Toad plopped down in a mud puddle. Woodpecker and Warbler lined up on a bough, and Coqui silently joined them.

"Welcome, friends," said Paz. "Listen. We are all becoming slothful. So I have decided to hold a race—with a wonderful secret prize."

Snake almost fell off her branch in surprise. Toad gasped and swallowed a mouthful of mud. The birds burst into the air with a wild beat of wings, and Coqui fell to the ground.

"See!" cried Paz. "There's life in us yet! The race will give us something to work toward. It will be held one moon from today."

Chattering broke out as the creatures tried to guess what the prize might be. Only Coqui, who had no voice, did not join in. Then everyone rushed off to prepare.

The creatures' laziness soon got the better of them, however, and bit by bit, everyone slid back into their lethargic ways.

All except Coqui. She saw her chance to beat the others. They laughed at the tiny frog's determination, but still she leaped, ran, and hopped every day until the day of the race.

The race began, and everyone took off. Snake was the first to fall behind, her breath hissing out of her. Next it was the birds, whose wings were not used to so much effort. Then Toad plopped to a stop, unable to hop any farther.

One by one, the creatures dropped out of the race, and so it was that only tiny Coqui crossed the finish line.

"Well done, Coqui!" Paz congratulated her. "For your prize, I will give you the one thing you want most of all."

All the creatures wished then that they had tried harder, but the prize was Coqui's. The thing that she wanted most of all was a voice!

And that is why, if you are ever in Puerto Rico at night, you will hear Coqui and all of her relations calling proudly from the trees, "Ko-kee, ko-kee, ko-kee."

Make Connections

Why do you think people create legends to explain nature or natural events? ESSENTIAL QUESTION

How are the stories *An Extraordinary Girl* and *How Coqui Got Her Song* similar? How are they different? TEXT TO TEXT

Focus on Genre

Tall Tales Tall tales are stories about people who have exaggerated abilities. These tales often highlight qualities that are valued in a culture, such as physical strength or self-confidence. Sometimes a tall tale is based on the life of a real person, but his or her feats are exaggerated beyond what could really be true.

Read and Find In *An Extraordinary Girl*, a baby has extraordinary abilities. As Sally Ann grows, her exploits become more and more incredible. These are described using exaggerated comparisons. For example, "Her roar sent the falling stars shooting back up into the sky and the rivers running back to where they came from." (page 6)

Your Turn

What abilities do you value? List at least five abilities. For example, you might list scoring well on computer games, soccer skills, and dance moves.

Next, for each one, write an exaggerated comparison to describe a person who has this ability. For example, "She could dribble that soccer ball right around the moon and back in the blink of an eye."

Illustrate one of your ideas and share it with the class.